Copyright © 2013 by Gelcys Iliana Basulto.

All rights reserved. No part of this book may be reproduced or transmitted in any form or by any means, electronic or mechanical, including photocopying, recording, or by any information storage and retrieval system, without permission in writing from the copyright owner.

This is a work of fiction. Names, characters, places and incidents either are the product of the author's imagination or are used fictitiously, and any resemblance to any actual persons, living or dead, events, or locales is entirely coincidental.

Rev. date: 10/05/2016

Giuliana is going to the park, but before she goes she must clean her playroom.

"I made such a big mess! Will you please help me clean it up?" Asked Giuliana.

"Oh look, my ABC flashcards! Do you know your ABCs?"

ABCDEFGHI

JKLMNOPQR

STUVWXYZ

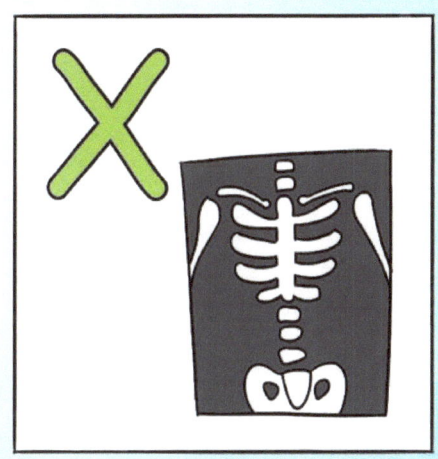

Giuliana is almost done cleaning up. "Look what else I found...my number cards! Can you count to ten with me?"

ONE, TWO, THREE, FOUR, FIVE...

1 ONE
2 TWO
3 THREE
4 FOUR
5 FIVE

SIX, SEVEN, EIGHT, NINE, TEN.

"I had fun cleaning my playroom with you today! Great counting and saying our ABCs...bye!"

www.ingramcontent.com/pod-product-compliance
Lightning Source LLC
LaVergne TN
LVHW072103070426
835508LV00002B/250